TWERK

ABCs of Holistic Birthing
& Comfort Measures to Support Birthing People

MELANIN ÀJẸ́ SESHAT

Copyright © 2021 by Melanin & Books
All rights reserved.

This book or any portion thereof may not be reproduced or
used in any manner whatsoever without the express written permission
of the publisher except for the use of brief quotations in a book review.

The information contained within this book is for educational purposes only
and should not be used as medical advice. This book is intended to be used in addition to
comprehensive prenatal care, doula support, and childbirth education.
Consult with a qualified care provider before implementing any of the tools discussed within this book.

Published in the United States of America by Melanin & Books.

First Edition, 2021 ISBN/SKU: 978-1-7379696-1-7

Publishing Date - 10/02/2021
Melanin & Books

Washington D.C.
www.thecannabisdoula.org

for Black girls who love to twerk

AFFIRMATIONS
ACUPRESSURE
ANANDAMIDE

Use **affirmations**, or affirmative statements, throughout pregnancy and during childbirth to manifest a beautiful birth experience. Incorporating the use of acupuncture and acupressure may provide natural relief to common pregnancy concerns including physical discomforts, nausea, and headaches. **Acupressure** is an ancient practice that involves applying pressure to specific points in the body, hand and feet, to release tension in the muscles and promote circulation of the blood. Acupressure utilizes massage and firm touch to balance energy throughout the body using counter-pressure to provide relief to physical discomforts while naturally boosting our anandamide levels. **Anandamide** is our *internal bliss molecule*, an endogenous cannabinoid made naturally in our bodies that produces feelings of joy, balance, and homeostasis. Boost your anandamide levels naturally with acupressure, acupuncture, or by eating apples!

BREASTFEEDING

Breastfeeding provides a lifetime of health benefits for both mom and baby. It also helps with bonding, empathy, and healthy attachments. Nursing within the first hour after birth, The Golden Hour, helps the uterus to contract by increasing oxytocin naturally, and provides baby with colostrum, human-milk rich in antibodies and essential nutrients. Breastfeeding, also known as chestfeeding, provides comfort to the mother, birthing person, and newborn after birth and is encouraged for the first two years of life. Nursing can be done using a bottle, pumping, hand-expressing, or using human milk from a donor. Breastfeeding may also reduce the chances of developing breast cancer later in life.

CHILDBIRTH CLASS
CHIROPRACTIC CARE
CANNABIS MEDICINE

Childbirth classes are essential to having an empowering birth experience, learning about birth options, and making informed decisions during pregnancy. There are childbirth classes that focus on natural births, comfort measures, newborn care, and there's even classes to support parents in making informed decisions on cannabis during pregnancy by The Cannabis Doula! **Cannabis medicine** has traditionally been used for centuries to support common pregnancy-related concerns such as nausea/vomiting, pain, inflammation, and mental health concerns, by providing support to our Endocannabinoid system. **Chiropractic care** also supports our ECS and can help bring our bodies into proper alignment and balance during pregnancy, alleviating common pregnancy and birth discomforts. Many birthing parents find chiropractic care essential to their prenatal and postpartum health and wellness.

DOULA

A **doula** is a birth professional who provides non-medical physical, mental, and emotional support during pregnancy, childbirth, and postpartum and various transitions in the lives of childbearing people. Full Circle Doulas support families in prenatal education, culturally-competent birth and postpartum support, preparing meals, supporting families with herbal remedies, mother blessings, belly binding, and other traditional and holistic birth practices. Having a doula reduces the chances of having an epidural or surgical birth, decreases discomfort, and leads to better birth outcomes.

EXERCISE

ENDOCANNABINOID SYSTEM (ECS)

Exercise during pregnancy helps to improve mood and mobility, reduce the chances of developing common pregnancy complications and risks such as preeclampsia and gestational diabetes, while helping to promote healthy weight gain, muscle tone, and endurance needed for a healthy childbirth. Exercise can also help to manage bloating/swelling during pregnancy, improve sleep, constipation, and back pain, and reduce the likelihood of medical interventions during childbirth. Moderate aerobic exercise for at least 30 minutes each day can include walking, swimming, bike riding, yoga, and is usually highly encouraged. Exercise supports our **Endocannabinoid System (ECS),** the grand conductor of all the other systems in our body, responsible for regulating our mood, memory, pain, and immune system, as well as pre- and post-pregnancy functions. Support your ECS to maintain a healthy pregnancy and birth.

FRESH FOODS
FRESH AIR
FOLATE

Fresh foods during pregnancy help to increase blood flow and help to provide the essential vitamins and nutrients needed for a healthy pregnancy and baby. Always look for organic fruits and vegetables. **Folate** is a B-vitamin essential for healthy growth and development, and is also known as folic acid in supplements and fortified foods. Naturally found in leafy greens, vegetables, fruit, nuts, and beans, folate has been proven to be particularly important for the development of the nervous system and for preventing birth defects in babies. **Fresh air** is also needed to support a healthy pregnancy by preventing the exposure to any harmful household chemicals, environmental toxins, and pollutants that may cause complications in pregnancy and in newborns. Fresh air, clean water, and organic foods are essential for healthy brain and body function, growth, and development.

GRANNY MIDWIVES

Granny Midwives, also referred to as Grand Midwives, were traditional African American midwives, herbalists, and healers who supported families in the U.S. during enslavement until the mid to late 20th century. They incorporated natural African remedies, herbs, healing practices, and traditions that provided holistic support to the birthing families, elders, and children at a time when Black people were not able to receive care in white hospitals. They provided education, parenting and life skills, cookings, cleaning, and care to nurture the mother, support the father, and celebrate the new baby, in both Black and white communities. We honor their legacy and reclaim the traditions of our foremothers in supporting Black maternal health, promoting family wellness, and care in Black communities.

HOMEBIRTH
HERBS
HYPNOSIS

A **homebirth** can provide families with the option of receiving quality, personalized prenatal care, and birth support in the safety of their home. Homebirths are just as safe, often safer, than birthing in a hospital. Whether receiving care from an experienced, or licensed, homebirth midwife or planning to birth unassisted, our bodies are just as capable of birthing a healthy baby at home. **Herbs** are traditionally used in teas, topicals, tinctures, and as essential oils to provide holistic relief during pregnancy and postpartum, and for various aliments. **Hypnosis** is a powerful meditation tool used to train our subconscious mind in managing discomforts and for general wellness. Medical-grade hypnosis can be used to alleviate discomfort, fear, and trauma for an easier childbirth.

INTUITION

Use your **intuition** to guide you throughout pregnancy and birth. Trust your instincts in supporting you in making decisions related to your health and your baby, during pregnancy, childbirth, and postpartum. Trust fully in you innate ability to give birth and your instincts as a parent. Decalcifying the pineal gland, practicing grounding, and detoxing our bodies help us to be better in tune with the infinite, the Creator, and all of the universe so that we may be guided in trusting our intuition.

JOY

Find joy in everything you do! **Joy** is a lasting state of happiness that is not relative; it is internal and not impacted by life's changes or fleeting moments. Fill your life with everything that brings you joy and peace, and release all that does not serve you. Practicing gratitude and living with joy can manifest into absolute happiness into our lives, minimizing stress and anxiety, especially during pregnancy through postpartum.

Radiate your joy outward and share it with others.

KEGELS

Kegels are exercises that strengthen the pelvic floor. Doing kegels regularly helps to strengthen the muscles that support the bladder, uterus, small intestines, and rectum. During pregnancy, kegels helps to prepare these muscles and the perineum for birth. After birth, kegels help to strengthen and tighten the vaginal muscles and perineum. Start by squeezing your pelvic floor muscles for 3 seconds, then release for 3 seconds. Do this 10 times in a row. Practice holding the muscles for up to 10 seconds, and release. Do multiple sets, and repeat daily.

LOVE & LAUGHTER

Love and laughter, especially during the birthing time, can help to increase oxytocin, the *love hormone*, and anandamide, our *internal bliss molecule,* which aids in a more pleasurable pregnancy and birth experience by naturally minimizing physical, mental, and emotional discomforts. For a healthy pregnancy, birth, and stress-free postpartum, fill your life and your surroundings with love, light, and laughter .

MIDWIFE

A **Midwife** is highly-skilled and trained medical professional who supports women and birthing families during pregnancy, childbirth, and postpartum, and provides reproductive care and wellness visits from menstruation through menopause. The midwifery model of care centers physiological births, promotes woman-centered care, and shared-decision making. Midwives can be found in hospitals, birth centers, and supporting families at homebirths. Black midwives provide exceptional care to Black birthing people and families during pregnancy and the first six-weeks after birth. Locate and hire a qualified midwife to support your family during pregnancy, birth, and postpartum.

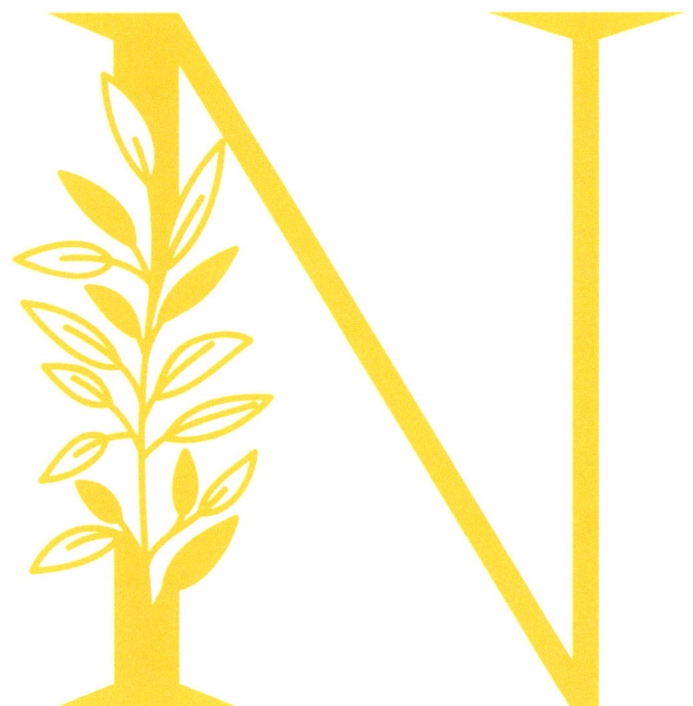

NURTURE

To **nurture** means to nourish, support, and provide empathetic and compassionate care in order to support healthy development and well-being. Nurturing Parenting is a trauma-informed, evidence-based parent education program that provides parents with tools and techniques to cultivate a nurturing family life environment and break generational curses related to domestic violence and childhood trauma.

To be nurturing parents, we must first nurture ourselves.

Oxytocin is the *love hormone!* During birth our natural levels of oxytocin increases to support parent-infant bonding, nursing, and acts to relieve mental, physical, and emotional discomforts. We can increase our oxytocin levels naturally during childbirth by having sex, nipple stimulation, kissing, massage, hugs and comforting touch, and by receiving compliments. Yoga, music, and meditation also increase oxytocin naturally. Synthetic oxytocin can cause complications during birth and postpartum, often leading to a cascade of medical interventions that routinely occur in hospitals, and should not be used with understanding these risks.

PRESSURE WAVES
PLACENTA

Pressure waves are physical sensations that prepare the uterus to birth the baby. These sensations of the uterus contracting usually wrap around the womb and can last between a few seconds on up to over a minute during active birth. They may be intense for some birthing people, however, they are necessary in facilitating the birthing progress. After the baby is born, pressure waves also help to birth the placenta. The **placenta** is an organ we make during pregnancy. It is the life-force sustaining our baby in the womb. The placenta provides nutrients to the baby, and works to filter toxins from mother to baby. Some cultural traditions include burying the placenta, encapsulating it, or consuming the placenta blended in smoothies or added in food, or tinctures. Consuming the placenta is said to provide relief from postpartum depression and restore nutrients to the birthing person.

QUIETUDE

Implement **quietude** in your wellness and pregnancy journey. Quiet time involves no music, no phones, no social media, no television. Our lives are filled with noise, especially living in crowded cities. Spend time alone, out in nature, and in silence; in calmness and tranquility. This helps to reset and promote balance, and peace.

Our little ones, especially, need quiet time each day. Use this time to rest, meditate, pray, and recenter. Practices like yoga, reading, writing, Tai chi and other Endocannabinoid wellness activities, coloring or painting, all make for great quiet and reflective activities.

RITUAL

Rituals are important to establish in our daily lives. They ground us and allow us to connect with the Creator and our highest selves. Rituals are often used by doulas and traditional midwives to provide spiritual support to the birthing families. Rituals can include sound bath healing, deep breathing, meditation, prayer, yoga, preparing a meal, or even going for a walk can be a ritual.

Create your own unique rituals to support your holistic health and wellness. Rituals are especially useful during pregnancy, childbirth, and early parenting.

SEX
SQUAT
SING

Sex can help naturally induce the start of birth by increasing our levels of oxytocin and softening the cervix. **Squatting** is the best position for birthing to help the baby descend into the pelvis. Squatting works with the flow of gravity and is a very comfortable position that people have always used to give birth naturally using a birth stool or birth ball for support. **Singing**, moaning, or vocalizing during birth, can also help to open the vagina by stimulating and opening the throat. Use sex, squatting, and singing to welcome your baby naturally. No induction necessary!

TWERK

Twerking is an African form of movement and dance that involves squatting, thrusting, and rotating the hips and booty, usually done to the beat of music. This cultural and collective dance is preformed across various African cultures and communities, as a celebration and expression of freedom, love, and joy. Twerking promotes womb healing and wellness using divine feminine energy.

Twerking throughout pregnancy, and during childbirth, is a great invigorating exercise for opening the hips and pelvis, positioning the baby in the pelvis, and can help birth to progress. T is for TWERK, TWERK, TWERK!

UTERUS

A healthy **uterus** is necessary for a healthy birth. The uterus is an internal reproductive organ, the womb, where the fetus develops during pregnancy. Support the health of your womb by eating mindfully, consuming healthy foods, drinking water, and avoiding uterine toxins like menstrual products made with dangerous chemicals, tampons, even partners with poor hygiene. Using herbs in yoni steaming, suppositories, and drinking teas, like raspberry leaf tea, can strengthen the uterus, and provide relief for many conditions of the uterus and the vagina.

VAGINA VIBRATOR

The **vagina** is a muscular canal that connects the uterus to the vulva, allowing for menstruation, sexual intercourse, and childbirth. Some may refer to the vaginal canal as a sacred path toward enlightenment and divine femininity because it leads to the uterus, the home to divine feminine intuition, spirituality, and consciousness. For this reason the use of the Sanskrit word, yoni, meaning *sacred space* is used intentionally in place of the word vagina. The vagina is naturally self-cleaning and self-lubricating.

A **vibrator**, used for massage, clitoral and vaginal stimulation, can be used during childbirth for pain relief and relaxation, to facilitate an orgasmic birth, and to naturally increasing the flow of oxytocin.

WOMB WATER BIRTH

Our **womb** is the center of our feminine intuition and health. Womb healing is a spiritual journey to heal the womb from past trauma related to sexual abuse, unhealthy relationships and attachments, toxic menstrual products and environmental toxins, infections, and other emotional traumas held in the womb. Womb healing can include meditation, journaling, changing diets, womb healing circles, cleanses, detoxing, and incorporating healthier birth practices.

A **water birth** is a gentle and peaceful way to give birth without the use of medication, usually at home or at a birth center. Water births provide relaxation and relief from discomfort using hydrotherapy while the newborn is able to more easily and peacefully transition outside of the womb.

X- RAY

X - rays, and ultrasounds, during pregnancy should only be used after thoughtful consideration and informed decision-making. They are safest when used only for serious medical concerns at a low frequency and for a short amount of time. X-rays, ultrasounds, and dopplers emit sound frequency waves that research suggests may be harmful to the developing fetus. Alternatively, a fetoscopes can be used to determine the position of the baby and the heartbeat. Exposure to microwave radiation in utero may also have a neurodevelopmentally toxic effect of the fetus. Be mindful of standing in front of the microwave during pregnancy to prevent risks of radiation, or exposure to radioactive waves. Not keeping cell phones on the body, belly, or laptops on the lap while pregnant are other mindful practices to incorporate to reduce the risks of long term affects to fertility, immune, and hormonal health due to electromagnetic radiation.

YONI STEAM
YOGA

Yoni steaming is a gentle, relaxing, and rejuvenating therapy that involves sitting or squatting over a pot of steaming herbs, or water, using a stool or steam sauna. The healing steam softens and relaxes the cervix allowing the herbal properties to permeate the yoni, the uterus; healing and supporting the perineum. Yoni steaming, or peristeam hydrotherapy, is used to help support a number of gynecological and emotional issues, and has been traditionally used for inducing childbirth and for postpartum healing.

Incorporating yoga into you daily life can also support womb health and overall well-being. **Yoga** is a physical exercise and spiritual practice that can be used to support physical and mental health, sexual healing, enlightenment, prenatal and postpartum wellness, and the little ones love it, too. Yoga naturally supports our body's Endocannabinoid System, creating harmony and homeostasis within our bodies!

ZEN & ZEAL

Zen is a Buddhist practice of emphasizing peace, calm, intuition, and meditation into ur daily lives. Living a life of zen helps to minimize stress that can lead to disease, illness, pregnancy complications, and postpartum depression.

To live a life of **zeal** is to be energized and motivated toward manifesting your dreams. Live life fervently with zen and zealously strive toward becoming your highest, most enlightened self while manifesting the birth that is most aligned with your mind, body, spirit, and cultural traditions.

Remember to TWERK for a natural birth.

- Time - Invest *time* into preparing for childbirth! It takes around 38-42 weeks to properly prepare for your mind, body, and spirit for childbirth. Baby will come when baby is ready. Be patient! Let your birth begin naturally.

- Water - Stay hydrated during pregnancy and throughout your birthing time. Drink at least 10 glasses to a gallon of fresh water each day. Using hot/cold water during childbirth, or having a water birth, can reduce birth discomforts and provide relaxation and hydrotherapy.

- Energy - Keep *positive + sacred energy* around you during pregnancy, and especially during your birthing time, to reduce stress and create balance for a more mindful and intentional birth experience.

- Rest - Rest throughout pregnancy. Rest in between pressure waves and early in your birthing time. Rest for the first 60 days after giving birth, and as much as you can in the first 1-2 years after giving birth. *Rest is revolutionary.* Adequate rest is necessary for nurturing parents.

- Knowledge - *Knowledge is power.* The more informed you are about pregnancy and childbirth, the better prepared you are in manifesting your birth and postpartum plan, making informed decisions, and the more empowered you will be in your pregnancy, birth, and parenting journey.

About TWERK

We grew up in Chicago with twerking as a form of self-expression and Black joy! I still vividly remember going to my first juke party in 5th grade, and detailing the experience in my journal. I was maybe twelve years old dancing in the kitchen drinking kool-aid when I was first shamed and punished for gyrating, as my parents called it then; an experience my family still likes to share! And again, in high school for juking at a homecoming party or two, and dancing too provocatively on the cheerleading team. While the stigma of Black women and girls moving our bodies always seem to provoke shaming from others who sexualize our bodies and our being, for me it has always been a way to release and celebrate sacred feminine energy and life. I see twerking as another form of praise dance, only outside the church. Whether twerking with the girls back in college, juking in high school, or pole dancing at home, twerking has empowered me in womb healing and wellness. I hope you find liberation, joy, and empowerment here, too.

Twerking is powerful.

Twerk daily! Before and during pregnancy, even during childbirth, to help open the pelvis and hips, and during postpartum to strengthen abdominal muscles. It is exercise for the womb and for the whole body. Twerking helped me birth two babies naturally! With music, as part of your morning routine, dancing with a partner, at a party, or in community with other women—twerking is revolutionary; a practice done by birthing women and girls since the beginning of time. So go forth, and twerk 'sum!

About the author
Melanin Ajé Seshat

Melanie Julion, B.S., HCHI, HCHD, LCCE, PFC
Founder/Creator of The Cannabis Doula, Inc.
Author of *The Cannabis Doula: The Transparent Enlightenment of My Own Rebirth*

I began my journey as a birthworker shortly after finding out I was pregnant with my first son, and even more intentionally after our accidental unassisted homebirth in 2016. I've been supporting youth and families in various capacities for 10+ years, graduating from Northern Illinois University in 2013 with a Bachelor of Science in Family & Child Studies and an emphasis in Family Social Services. Who knew a "mom-degree" could be add so much value to my life and my community!? I'm a mama to two toddlers, both of whom had very beautiful, peaceful, natural births. Early in my journey I began supporting primarily cannabis-consuming families, Black women, close friends and family, which has wildly shaped my mission in providing culturally-competent, evidence-based care to Black communities. I am proudly trained as a SMC Full Circle Doula, DONA-trained Birth Doula, and Hypnobabies HypnoDoula. As a doula, I support families from early pregnancy through postpartum, providing holistic and herbal support rooted in the legacy of African American birth traditions. I'm especially passionate about childbirth education and family life education. I'm a Lamaze Certified Childbirth Educator, Hypnobabies Childbirth Hypnosis Instructor, and Nurturing Parenting Facilitator with several certifications in cannabis medicine. It has been a joy serving my community in the capacity that I have.

I've had the wonderful honor of supporting and educating expectant families and doulas from all over the country, and internationally, from various backgrounds and cultures through The Cannabis Doula! I'm a Chicago girl based in Washington D.C., where you'll likely catch me at the drum circle at Malcolm X park, supporting clients, reading and exploring nature with my little ones.

www.ingramcontent.com/pod-product-compliance
Lightning Source LLC
Chambersburg PA
CBHW041648160426

43209CB00019B/1855